Books by W. S. Merwin

POEMS

Opening the Hand 1983
Finding the Islands 1982
The Compass Flower 1977
The First Four Books of Poems 1975
(INCLUDING THE COMPLETE TEXTS OF
A Mask for Janus, The Dancing Bears,
Green with Beasts AND *The Drunk in the Furnace*)
Writings to an Unfinished Accompaniment 1973
The Carrier of Ladders 1970
The Lice 1967
The Moving Target 1963
The Drunk in the Furnace 1960
Green With Beasts 1956
The Dancing Bears 1954
A Mask for Janus 1952

PROSE

Unframed Originals 1982
Houses and Travellers 1977
The Miner's Pale Children 1970

TRANSLATIONS

Selected Translations 1968–1978 1979
Osip Mandelstam, Selected Poems
(WITH CLARENCE BROWN) 1974
Asian Figures 1973
Transparence of the World (Poems by Jean Follain) 1969
Voices (Poems by Antonio Porchia) 1969
Products of the Perfected Civilization
(Selected Writings of Chamfort) 1969
Twenty Love Poems and a Song of Despair
(Poems by Pablo Neruda) 1969
Selected Translations 1948–1968 1968
The Song of Roland 1963
Lazarillo de Tormes 1962
The Satires of Persius 1960
Spanish Ballads 1960
The Poem of the Cid 1959

The Compass Flower

The Compass Flower

POEMS BY **W. S. Merwin**

New York ATHENEUM *1983*

The following poems were originally published in THE NEW YORKER: Fishing; Guardians; On the Mountain; Vision; City; The Estuary; The Counting Houses; Numbered Apartment; St Vincent's; Summer Night on the Stone Barrens; Memory of Summer Facing West; The Love for October; Autumn Evening; Kore; Spring Equinox Full Moon; Late Snow; June Rain; The Coin.

Other poems were originally published in HUDSON REVIEW; MUNDUS ARTIUM; HARPER'S; THE GEORGIA REVIEW; KAYAK; THE ATLANTIC MONTHLY; BELOIT POETRY JOURNAL; TIMES LITERARY SUPPLEMENT; FIELD; ANTAEUS; PARIS REVIEW; CHOICE; THE ANTIOCH REVIEW; THE NATION; THE OHIO REVIEW.

I wish to thank the Guggenheim Foundation for a grant on which I was living when this book was begun. W.S.M.

Library of Congress Cataloging in Publication Data:

Merwin, William S 1927–
The compass flower.

I. Title.
PS3563.E75C6 811'.5'4 76-27345
ISBN 0-689-10768-4

Published simultaneously in Canada by McClelland and Stewart Ltd
Manufactured by Fairfield Graphics, Fairfield, Pennsylvania
Designed by Harry Ford
First printing January 1977
Second printing September 1977
Third printing September 1980
Fourth printing May 1983

for Dana

Contents

I

II

III

I V

I

THE HEART

In the first chamber of the heart
all the gloves are hanging but two
the hands are bare as they come through the door
the bell rope is moving without them
they move forward cupped as though
holding water
there is a bird bathing in their palms
in this chamber there is no color

In the second chamber of the heart
all the blindfolds are hanging but one
the eyes are open as they come in
they see the bell rope moving
without hands
they see the bathing bird
being carried forward
through the colored chamber

In the third chamber of the heart
all the sounds are hanging but one
the ears hear nothing as they come through the door
the bell rope is moving like a breath
without hands
a bird is being carried forward
bathing
in total silence

In the last chamber of the heart
all the words are hanging
but one
the blood is naked as it steps through the door
with its eyes open
and a bathing bird in its hands

and with its bare feet on the sill
moving as though on water
to the one stroke of the bell
someone is ringing without hands

THE WINE

With what joy I am carrying
a case of wine up a mountain
far behind me others
are being given their burdens
but I could not wait even for them

it is wine that I will not drink
I will not drink it not I
this wine
a signpost is swinging around
up in the woods in the fog
one way saying Almost one way Punished
in another language that I know
but no sign this way

by now all the stone railing
is fog
no longer does the dew brushed
from the pine needles onto my fingers
run down into my armpits
how cold my hands are
how awkward the wine is to carry
on my shoulder
that's part of the joy

THE DRIVE HOME

I was always afraid
of the time when I would arrive home
and be met by a special car
but this wasn't like that
they were so nice the young couple
and I was relieved not to be driving
so I could see the autumn leaves on the farms

I sat in the front to see better
they sat in the back
having a good time
and they laughed with their collars up
they said we could take turns driving
but when I looked
none of us was driving

then we all laughed
we wondered if anyone would notice
we talked of getting an inflatable
driver
to drive us for nothing through the autumn leaves

THE NEXT MOON

A month to the hour
since the last ear on earth
heard your voice

even then on the phone

I know the words about rest
and how you would say them
as though I myself had heard them
not long ago
but for a month I have heard nothing

and in the evening after the moon of deafness
I set foot in the proud waters
of iron and misfortune
it is a month to the hour
since you died
and it was only dusk
to the east in the garden

now it is a night street with another moon
seen for the first time but no longer new
and faces from the backs of mirrors

THE SNOW

You with no fear of dying
how you dreaded winter
the cataract forming on the green wheated hill
ice on sundial and steps and calendar
it is snowing
after you were unborn it was my turn
to carry you in a world before me
trying to imagine you
I am your parent at the beginning of winter
you are my child
we are one body
one blood
one red line melting the snow
unbroken line in falling snow

THE ARRIVAL

From many boats
ferries and borrowed canoes
white steamers and resurrected hulls
in which we were young together
to a shore older than waiting
and our feet on the wet shadowed sand
early in the evening of every verb
both of us at the foot of the mountain laughing

now will you lead me with the smell of almonds
up over the leafless mountain
in the blood red evening
now we pull up the keel through the rushes
on the beach
my feet miss the broken bottle
half buried in the sand
you did not notice it at last

now will you lead with your small hand
your child up the leafless mountain
past the green wooden doors thrown away
and abandoned shelters
into the meadows of loose horses
that I will ride in the dark to come

APPLES

Waking beside a pile of unsorted keys
in an empty room
the sun is high

what a long jagged string of broken bird song
they must have made as they gathered there
by the ears deaf with sleep
and the hands empty as waves
I remember the birds now
but where are the locks

when I touch the pile
my hand sounds like a wave on a shingle beach
I hear someone stirring
in the ruins of a glass mountain
after decades

those keys are so cold that they melt at my touch
all but the one
to the door of a cold morning
the colors of apples

AN ENCAMPMENT AT MORNING

A migrant tribe of spiders
spread tents at dusk in the rye stubble
come day I see the color
of the planet under their white-beaded tents
where the spiders are bent
by shade fires in damp September
to their live instruments
and I see the color of the planet
when their tents go from above it
as I come that way in a breath cloud
learning my steps
among the tents rising invisibly like the shapes of snowflakes
we are words on a journey
not the inscriptions of settled people

MIGRATION

Prayers of many summers come
to roost on a moment
until it sinks under them
and they resume their journey
flying by night
with the sound
of blood rushing in an ear

NOVEMBER

The landscape
of a link disappearing between species
and phyla
and kingdoms
is here
after what we have said good-bye to
and before what we will not be here to see
only we know this
as we are
the earth sealed with tar
the walls climbing
the feathers warm around the heart
the memory of unmarked woods
standing facing something we cannot see
exchanging familiar speech
archaic greetings of those who reappear

THE HORSE

In a dead tree
there is the ghost of a horse
no horse
was ever seen near the tree
but the tree was born
of a mare
it rolled with long legs
in rustling meadows
it pricked its ears
it reared and tossed its head
and suddenly stood still
beginning to remember
as its leaves fell

A CONTEMPORARY

What if I came down now out of these
solid dark clouds that build up against the mountain
day after day with no rain in them
and lived as one blade of grass
in a garden in the south when the clouds part in winter
from the beginning I would be older than all the animals
and to the last I would be simpler
frost would design me and dew would disappear on me
sun would shine through me
I would be green with white roots
feel worms touch my feet as a bounty
have no name and no fear
turn naturally to the light
know how to spend the day and night
climbing out of myself
all my life

FISHING

Day and night as a child
I could imagine feeling the bite on the line
moment of fire
above a drum of white
stone water
with the line vibrating through it
one-string harp
never to be out of the feeling in my fingers
name from before anyone was born
bright color in darkness through half a life
beating suddenly toward me

GUARDIANS

Fine rain drifts along mountains to the south of me
graying the first month
one migrant bird scolding in misted noon
in the pear tree
dogs yapping beyond mud walls
echoing back and forth wooden bells
who is listening
eight sacred fears keep watch over me
behind each of them one of the porches of dissolution
in the place of the ninth an open gate
each of them holds the end of one strand
of a rope made of the eight ribs of the world
which leads through the fearless gate

the swan drifts over mountains to the south of me
in the first month
and in the white cloud small birds begin to sing
hair-roots of trees stir
fear is one aspect of joyful guardians
because of the way I came
and clearly I have been in love with some of them
with her who is Fear of the Journey
who has repeatedly and faithfully led me
most of them I cannot even see
in the white sky over my travelling cradle
watching me
ready to bear me up in ageless hands
of cloud and glass
for as long as I need them

FATE

Cloud in the morning
evening a white opal
after a white sun
the lighted opal sits on the rim
of dark mountains
some are born hearing dogs bark in the mountains
among high walls just after sunset
and all their lives things are known to them
that are not known even to those born hearing water
or trees or sobbing or flutes or laughing

ON THE MOUNTAIN

A wind at first light
comes out of one
waving pine tree
air river too deep to be seen
current with no surface
then can be heard and felt
it carries deep reflections of birds
and of sunrise clouds
thoughts into the sea of day

VISION

What is unseen
flows to what is unseen
passing in part
through what we partly see
we stood up from all fours
far back in the light
to look
as long as there is day
and part of the night

THE DELUGE

Before there was a body
an eye wandered in a forest
to see how it would be
only when the trees were gone
did the veins appear
newly joined and windowed
and the eye embarked in the body
one of an only pair
on the rising waters
to watch for the end of the rain
of age

ROBIN

In one of the creations
the robin invented
the day
in order to escape from the owl
and they
killed cock robin
and he entered the next world
when the world he knew was utterly destroyed
many worlds before ours
and he invented the day
for a new reason
and again we survived
we survivors
without knowing why

II

CITY

I have been here before
I have entered through a glass door
at the end of a corridor
surprised to find nothing locked
but knowing that someone was watching
I have arrived through a hospital
I have steered in through the tightening outskirts
in the morning crowd
I have undergone inspections been counted have believed
I have learned the streets like seasons
I have forgotten whole years
but never have I seen it with so few people showing
not even at this hour before daylight so little traffic
never so like held breath
all the traffic lights dark
never such temptation to drive too fast

LINE

Those waiting in line
for a cash register at a supermarket
pushing wire baby carriages
full of food in packages
past signs about coupons
in the blank light
do not look at each other
frankly
pretend not to stare at each other's
soft drinks and white bread
do not think of themselves as
part of a line
ordinarily
and the clerk often does not
look at them
giving them change
and the man who puts the things
they have chosen
into bags
talks to the clerk
as he never talks to her
at any other time

THE ESTUARY

By day we pace the many decks
of the stone boat
and at night we are turned out in its high windows
like stars of another side
taste our mouths we are the salt of the earth
salt is memory
in storm and cloud
we sleep in fine rigging like riding birds
taste our fingers
each with its own commandment
day or night it is harder to know than we know
but longer
we are asleep over charts at running windows
we are asleep with compasses in our hands
and at the bow of the stone boat
the wave from the ends of the earth keeps breaking

THE ROCK

Saxophone and subway
under waking and sleeping
then few hundred feet down nobody

sound of inner stone
with heart on fire

on top of it where it would dream
in the light on its head
and in its shadow
we know one another
riding deaf together
flying up in boxes
through gray gasses
and here pause
to breathe

all
our walls shake if we
listen
if we stop even
to rest a hand on them

when we can love it happens here too
where we tremble
who also are running like white grass
where sirens bleed through us
wires reach to us
we are bottles smashing in paper bags
and at the same time live standing in many windows
hearing under the breath the stone
that is ours alone

THE COUNTING HOUSES

Where do the hours of a city begin and end
among so many
the limits rising
and setting each time in each body
in a city how many hands of timepieces
must be counting the hours
clicking at a given moment
numbering insects into machines to be codified
calculating newsprint in the days of the living
all together they are not infinite
any more than the ignored patience
of rubber tires day and night
or the dumbness of wheels or the wires of passions

where is the horizon the avenue has not reached it
reaching and reaching lying palm upward
exposing the places where blood is given or let
at night the veins of the sleepers remember trees
countless sleepers the hours of trees
the uncounted hours the leaves in the dark
by day the light of the streets is the color of arms kept covered
and of much purpose
again at night the lights of the streets play on ceilings
they brush across walls
of room after unlit room hung with pictures
of the youth of the world

THE HELMSMEN

The navigator of day
plots his way by a few
daytime stars
which he never sees
except as black calculations
on white paper
worked out to the present
and even beyond
on a single plane
while on the same breathing voyage
the other navigator steers only
by what he sees
and he names for the visions of day
what he makes out in the dark void
over his head
he names for what he has never seen
what he will never see
and he never sees
the other
the earth itself is always between them
yet he leaves messages
concerning celestial bodies
as though he were telling of his own life
and in turn he finds
messages concerning
unseen motions of celestial bodies
movements of days of a life
and both navigators call out
passing the same places as the sunrise
and the sunset
waking and sleeping they call
but can't be sure whether they hear
increasingly they imagine echoes

year after year they
try to meet
thinking of each other constantly
and of the rumors of resemblances between them

NUMBERED APARTMENT

In every room rubber bands turn up loose
on dusty surfaces
witnesses

travellers in stopover countries
not knowing a word of the language
each of them
something in particular to do with me
who say laughing that I
was born here one William
on the last day of one September

to whom now it is again a January a Thursday
of an eleven year and
who has forgotten that
day and to whom that week is inaccessible
and this one is plain this
one

and though I say
here
I know it was not
for even at that time it was
ninety-nine streets to the north by the river
and now it is three wars back
and parents gone as though at once

the edifice in the antique
mode of kings of France
to which they took her to give birth
torn down as I
in my name was turning forty-four
and the building did not from that age go alone

into pieces wheeled away
but all through these years
rubber bands have continued to come to me
sometimes many together
arriving to accompany me although
the whole country has changed
means of travel accelerated
signs almost totally replaced traffic re-routed every
love altered
the stamps re-issued and
smells of streets and apples
moved on

the stone city in
the river has changed and of course
the river
and all words even those unread in
envelopes
all those shining cars vanished
after them entire roads gone like kite strings
incalculable records' print grown finer
just the names at that followed by smoke of numbers
and high buildings turned to glass in
other air oh one clear day

I am a different
foot of a same person in the same river
yet rubber bands lead to me and
from me across great distances
I do not recognize them coming nor remember them going
and still they continue to find me and pass like starlight

ST VINCENT'S

Thinking of rain clouds that rose over the city
on the first day of the year

in the same month
I consider that I have lived daily and with
eyes open and ears to hear
these years across from St Vincent's Hospital
above whose roof those clouds rose

its bricks by day a French red under
cross facing south
blown-up neo-classic facades the tall
dark openings between columns at
the dawn of history
exploded into many windows
in a mortised face

inside it the ambulances have unloaded
after sirens' howling nearer through traffic on
Seventh Avenue long
ago I learned not to hear them
even when the sirens stop

they turn to back in
few passers-by stay to look
and neither do I

at night two long blue
windows and one short one on the top floor
burn all night
many nights when most of the others are out
on what floor do they have
anything

I have seen the building drift moonlit through geraniums
late at night when trucks were few
moon just past the full
upper windows parts of the sky
as long as I looked
I watched it at Christmas and New Year
early in the morning I have seen the nurses ray out through
arterial streets
in the evening have noticed internes blocks away
on doorsteps one foot in the door

I have come upon the men in gloves taking out
the garbage at all hours
piling up mountains of
plastic bags white strata with green intermingled and
black
I have seen one pile
catch fire and studied the cloud
at the ends of the jets of the hoses
the fire engines as near as that
red beacons and
machine-throb heard by the whole body
I have noticed molded containers stacked outside
a delivery entrance on Twelfth Street
whether meals from a meal factory made up with those
mummified for long journeys by plane
or specimens for laboratory
examination sealed at the prescribed temperatures
either way closed delivery

and approached faces staring from above
crutches or tubular clamps
out for tentative walks
have paused for turtling wheel-chairs
heard visitors talking in wind on each corner

while the lights changed and
hot dogs were handed over at the curb
in the middle of afternoon
mustard ketchup onions and relish
and police smelling of ether and laundry
were going back

and I have known them all less than the papers of our days
smoke rises from the chimneys do they have an incinerator
what for
how warm do they believe they have to maintain the air
in there
several of the windows appear
to be made of tin
but it may be the light reflected
I have imagined bees coming and going
on those sills though I have never seen them

who was St Vincent

THE SHUTTLES

Remembering glitter on the first river
I begin to imagine the chances against
any fabric ever occurring
threads at last becoming original torn cloth
night numberless with lights
flying apart in galaxies I reach out
to imagine becoming one anything
once
among the chances in the rare
aging fabric happening
all the way for the first time

III

THE VINEYARD

—for Bill Matthews

Going up through the hill called the vineyard
that seems nothing but stone
you come to a tangle of wild plum and hazel bushes
the spring in the cliff like the sex of a green woman
the taste of the water
and of the stone

you come to the fox's cave in the yellow clay
under the foot of the stone
and barely out of reach lime-crusted nests
of swallows
and in the cliff higher up
holes of swifts and bees
solitary grass

all that stone faces southward
and a little to the east
full of crevices
bats and small birds
foxes and wild honey
clear to the top they call it
the vineyard
where earliest the light
is seen that bids the cock crow

CROSSING PLACE

I crossed the stream
on the rocks
in the summer
evening
trying not to spill
the pitcher of water
from the falls

SUMMER NIGHT ON THE STONE BARRENS

In the first hours of darkness
while the wide stones are still warm from the sun
through the hush waiting for thunder
a body falls out of a tree
rat or other soft skin
one beat of one heart on the bare stone
gets up and runs on
lightning flaps on the lifted horizon
both scattered beyond black leaves
nearby different cricket notes
climb and the owl cries
the worn moon will rise late among clouds
unseen larks rang at sunset
over yellow thistles of that day
I am under the ancient roof alone
the beams are held up by forgotten builders
of whom there were never pictures
I love voices not heard
but I love them
from some of them with every breath
I go farther away
and to some I return even through storm and sleep
the stillness is a black pearl
and I can see into it while the animals fall
one at a time at immeasurable intervals

SEPTEMBER PLOWING

For seasons the walled meadow
south of the house built of its stone
grows up in shepherd's purse and thistles
the weeds share April as a secret
finches disguised as summer earth
click the drying seeds
mice run over rags of parchment in August
the hare keeps looking up remembering
a hidden joy fills the songs of the cicadas

two days' rain wakes the green in the pastures
crows agree and hawks shriek with naked voices
on all sides the dark oak woods leap up and shine
the long stony meadow is plowed at last and lies
all day bare
I consider life after life as treasures
oh it is the autumn light

that brings everything back in one hand
the light again of beginnings
the amber appearing as amber

WORKING INTO AUTUMN

Daylight clears after rain to show cool morning
pools in the stones echo birds' water-songs
new growth is washed on tall trees before the leaves turn
hens stray across empty pastures jays ignore them
gliding over them onto the glittering grass laughing
yesterday toward sunset horizon clouds parted
and mosquitoes sailed in glass rain by the open window
where I remained the distance came to me
all day I caulk a house to launch it at nightfall

MEMORY OF SUMMER FACING WEST

Sheep and rocks drifting together before sunset
late birds rowing home across bright spaces
shadows stroking the long day above the earth
wild voices high and far-carrying
at sun's descent toward ripening grain

THE LOVE FOR OCTOBER

A child looking at ruins grows younger
but cold
and wants to wake to a new name
I have been younger in October
than in all the months of spring
walnut and may leaves the color
of shoulders at the end of summer
a month that has been to the mountain
and become light there
the long grass lies pointing uphill
even in death for a reason
that none of us knows
and the wren laughs in the early shade now
come again shining glance in your good time
naked air late morning
my love is for lightness
of touch foot feather
the day is yet one more yellow leaf
and without turning I kiss the light
by an old well on the last of the month
gathering wild rose hips
in the sun

AUTUMN EVENING

In the late day shining cobwebs trailed from my fingers
I could not see the far ends somewhere to the south
gold light hung for a long time in the wild clematis
called old man's beard along the warm wall
now smoke from my fire drifts across the red sun setting
half the bronze leaves still hold to the walnut trees
marjoram joy of the mountains flowers again
even in the light frosts of these nights
and there are mushrooms though the moon is new
and though shadows whiten on the grass before morning
and cowbells sound in the dusk from winter pastures

KORE

α I have watched your smile in your sleep
and I know it is the boat
in which my sun rides under the earth
all night on the wave of your breath
no wonder the days grow short
and waking without you
is the beginning of winter

β How is it that I can hear your bird voice now
trickling among the ice towers
through the days of the anvil
as the year turns I carry an echo
over my own stones and I listen
my eyes are open looking ahead
I walk a little ahead of myself touching
the light air where nobody sees you
and the sun as it sets through the forest of windows
unrolls slowly its
unrepeatable secret
all the colors of autumn without the leaves

γ You were shaking and an air full of leaves
flowed out of the dark falls of your hair
down over the rapids of your knees
until I touched you and you grew quiet
and raised to me
your hands and your eyes and showed me
twice my face burning in amber

δ Already on the first hill with you beside me
at the foot of the ruins I saw through the day
and went on without pausing
loving the unheld air
as a wing might love it flying
toward you unknowing
knowing

ϵ Face that I loved when I was a child
nobody in that age believed us
when we said we would go away together
not even when we said that the flood
was on its way
and nobody will find us when it is over

ζ You slept all the way to the garden
face in the boat of my hand
and we came more than a century late
to the closed gate
and the song the laurel remembers in the dark
the night flute always beginning again
on the untrodden slope
and where we walked in the streets then there was new wine
announced with green boughs over doorways
in the time of the statues

η Climbing at noon by roofless columns
with the day white on the sea
I did not know the word for the hour
nor for the hunger
nor for your hand
which I was not touching
but could feel in the air
The beginning
comes from before
when the words for it were pictures of strangers
it comes on wings that never waited for their names

θ In the house at the end of a day of rain the old man
began to recite a poem
no one remembered but everyone wanted to
only before he had finished it he lay down
taking the rest of it with him to sleep
then in the next light after my night's journey
you were running in leaves across a wide street
as I was running
and we had arrived

ι When they are together our hands are of an age
and a dark light flows up between them
into its feathers
We have brought
nothing with us
but what has come of itself
we pass the stone fragments
the ancient smiles holding out
no hands
like the trees their sisters born older

κ Autumn is one of the four elements
the air has four seasons strung
to its instrument
each with its own wind
but one note under them   Full moon   The year
has turned in the leafless veins
and the poles of the earth have sounded
I wake looking east hearing
the snow fall and your
feet far from here bare
climbing an untold stair
Long before sunrise hands of a child carrying grapes

λ At the top of the veins I hear
the finger on the bowstring
I hear my feet continuing
upward I hear you
hair in wind
I learn from you of the bare slope
where you are nowhere in sight
so we climb the mountain together after all
even with it between us

μ The candles flutter on the stairs of your voice
gold in the dark
and for this
far time you laughed through your whole childhood
and all those years my beloved spiders
guarded the treasure under my house
unlit until the night before you appeared

ν I have loved you in the four capitals
of four worlds before this one
with its glass season
and the nakedness of their light
wakes me now
and the burning that the year comes back for
leaping the falls of its own
changes

ξ The sun yellows pages of print
a snow of bats swirls in the streets
distractions
what I thought I knew falls aside a thought at a time
until I see you naked
in your eyes the bronze ferns older than seeing
unfurling above the dark springs

ο In winter far from you
at the thought of your skin
leaves
yet to be
stir in the sleep of roots
the tree
of veins trembles
at a distance and begins
gathering in secret the Sibyl's rustling

π I trust neither memory nor expectation
but even the white days of cities
belong to what they do not see
even the heart of the doubters' light is gold
even when you are not with me
in the flowerless month of the door god
you look at me with your eyes of arrival

ρ I found you the bracelets of plaited straw
you found me the old tools
that I had been looking for
you knew where they were
in my garden
few are the words for finding
as I told you under the beating flights
of autumn
and will tell you again
as I find them

σ We came to the red stone
that they call black in that country
because it fell out of the night
before anyone was there
and it floated ahead of us on the earth
alone without a shadow
but the night had not forgotten it
and its memory even then was falling after it
out of the future
past us into that day

τ Morning to morning
the same door opening inward
from both sides
laugh close as you are
it is cold in the house
and I burned up all the matches in the night
to look at you

υ Wire trees
days with telephones
pronouncing into black lamps
trying to get them to light
rubbing them
you appear in a gray street
having heard nothing
expecting nothing
with the light behind you
and our shadows burn the buildings

φ Thirty days after the solstice
forms of ripe wheat
emerge from the tips of the branches
Far outside them
here
where you have never been
I reach for you with my eyes
I call you with my body
that knows your one name

χ Days when I do not hear you
it seems that the season flows backward
but it is only
I
of hollow streets
deaf smoke
rain on water

ψ We cross the smooth night lake together
in the waiting boat
we are welcomed without lights
again and again we emerge by day
hand in hand
from all four corridors at once
under the echoing dome
guided by what has not been said

ω The shadow of my moving foot
feels your direction
you come toward me
bringing the gold through the rust
you step to me through the city of amber
under the moon and the sun
voice not yet in the words
what is spoken is already
another year

PASSAGE

In autumn in this same life
I was leaving a capital
where an old animal
captured in its youth
one that in the wild
would never have reached such an age
was watching the sun set
over nameless
unapproachable trees
and it is spring

IN THE PASS

Eleven horsemen gather at the hollow bridge
the light is cold and a snowy wind is blowing
the waterfall crashes and the stream below it
is bounding over the rocks under the ice
white spray has crusted on the planks
each of the horsemen as he rounds the cliff
and the bridge comes in sight
thinks of a bird and a woman
and dismounts and leads his horse over
into the spring and the blossoming valley
they are all the same horseman
falcon
mango-daughter

SPRING EQUINOX FULL MOON

I breathe to you
love in the south in the many
months of spring
hibiscus in dark hair water
at the source
shadows glistening to hips
thighs slender sunset shining shores

fingers rolled fragrant leaves
presence of deep woods
earth veiled in green drift
that hides running
of small airs
untraceable fine sounds
passing as on a face
feet first drops of rain on a mountain
hands greeting flowers
holding stolen flowers

closed eyes of every creature
sepia and amber days
back
of tall tree
arms' glide
voice of rain forests
birds in tree heights
throat of palm

wrist of palm
palm of palm
fruit nakedness
morsel breasts
melon navel waist of high waterfall

Spring Equinox Full Moon

surf laughter face hearing music
body of flight
secret
beach

away from you on a corner of the earth
I want to think for six hours of your hair
which is the invention of singing
daughter of islands
born in the flood of the fish harvest
I see long mornings
lying on your hair
I remember looking for you

THE MORNING

The first morning
I woke in surprise to your body
for I had been dreaming it
as I do

all around us white petals had never slept
leaves touched the early light
your breath warm as your skin on my neck
your eyes opening

smell of dew

SUMMER DOORWAY

I come down from the gold mountains
each of them the light of many years
high up the soughing of cold pines among stones
the whole way home dry grass seething
to these sounds I think of you already there
in the house all my steps lead to

you have the table set to surprise me
you are lighting the two candles
I come to the door quickly to surprise you
but you laugh we laugh you run toward me
under the long skirt your feet are bare
I drop to my knees in the doorway and catch you
holding the backs of your thighs I watch the candle flames
over my head you watch the birds flying home from the sea

THE HOSTS

You asked what
were the names of those two
old people who lived under the big tree
and gods in disguise visited them though they were poor

they offered the best they had to eat
and opened the oldest wine in the house
the gods went on pouring out pouring out wine
and then promised that it would flow till the ends of their lives

when the shining guests were out of sight he turned to her
by the table and said
this bottle has been in the cave all the time
we have been together

ISLANDS

Wherever I look you are islands
a constellation of flowers breathing on the sea
deep-forested islands mountainous and fragrant
fires on a bright ocean
at the root one fire

all my life I have wanted to touch your ankle
running down to its shore
I beach myself on you
I listen
I see you among still leaves
regard of rock pool
by sun and moon and stars

island waterfalls and their echoes
are your voice your shoulders the whole of you standing
and you turn to me as though your feet were in mist
flowers birds same colors
as your breath
the flowers deliberately smell of you
and the birds make their feathers
not to fly but to
feel of you

MOUNTAIN DAY

With one dear friend we go up the highest mountain
thousands of feet into the birdless snow
and listen to our breaths in the still air
for a long time beside the observatories
later we stretch out on the dark crumbled
lava slope looking
west at the sun yellowing the clouds below
then go down past the wild cows to the cabin
getting there just before sunset
and eat by the fire laughing at what we have
forgotten to bring
afterwards we come out and lie
braided together looking up
at Cassiopeia over the foothill

SNOWLINE

Turning climbing slowly in late spring among
black trunks of high pines
talking of our lives few white words flying
up into fringed boughs
unexpectedly we catch sight
across an immeasurable valley
of the long peak capped with snow and slanting light
that we saw far above us at morning
now appears scarcely higher than we are
cloud-cliff of moonlight by day
standing still we feel we could touch it
days distant in gleaming air
then we see footsteps of snow climbing all around us
into white sky

TWILIGHT

Oh you are never tame
fire on a mountain
eyes beside water
first day of petals

lying across the bed
in afternoon rainlight
arms of evening
wherever we are is a shore

LATE SNOW

Wallflowers leaping on slope facing southeast
steep waves glittering
three weeks in spring mountain winds
sweetvetch beardtongue bluebells
skyflowers
thimbleberry blossoming like a rose
white of catching all near sunlight
cold rain two days on long sparse mountain grass
darkening lichened boulders under pine trees
once we wake and it has snowed everywhere
from the railing you wave your arms to the pines
they are holding white sky above white ground
their own feet still sleeping in dark forest
birds shaking few pieces of day from boughs
in white cloud hushed light through canyon
feather sounds
snow falls into your dark hair

JUNE RAIN

The rain of the white valley the clear rain
the rain holding the whole valley while it falls
the mountain rain the high rain onto the mountain
as it rained on the mountain on the night we met
the many days' rain shadowless rain
blowing from the long eaves to go on falling
the rain whose ancestors
with no names
made the valley
the nameless shining rain whose past lives
made all the valleys
the author of the rivers
with unchanged and final voice
the rain that falls in the new open streams
running down the dirt roads on the mountain
the rain falling hour after hour into summer
the unexpected rain the long surprise
the rain we both watch at the same window
the rain we lie and listen to together
the rain we hear returning through the night
the rain we do not hear
the open rain

WHITE SUMMER FLOWER

Nameless

white poppy
whoever looks at you is alone

when I look at your petals
each time they open

and think of each time
that I have passed them

I know that I have wanted
to say Wait

and why should they

TREES

I am looking at trees
they may be one of the things I will miss
most from the earth
though many of the ones that I have seen
already I cannot remember
and though I seldom embrace the ones I see
and have never been able to speak
with one
I listen to them tenderly
their names have never touched them
they have stood round my sleep
and when it was forbidden to climb them
they have carried me in their branches

GRASS BEGINNING JULY

A pause at the top of a leap
a pause in the sun
itself as we say
east wind drifts up the steep hillside
on the mountain the heat of noon
has dried the full-grown
manes of the grass
the late-running herds
they run among the yucca
the deer-browsed yucca
yellow daisies cactus flowers
they run past rocks waiting on the slope
and prayer flag clothes drying
on the way to the trees
all of us moving together

IV

THE COIN

I have been to a fair alone
and across the river from the tented marketplace
and the church
were the green sagging balconies from which
during the occupation
the bodies of many
of the men of the town
hung for days in full view
of the women who had been their wives
I watched men in long
black coats selling animals
I watched money going
to a fat woman in white
who held pieces of white cheese
wrapped in white paper
out into the sunlight
I watched an old woman selling cut flowers
counting change
I looked at her teeth and lips
the dark kerchief on her head
there were carnations and
summer flowers rolled in wet newspaper
I considered the wares of a man
with a pile of whetstones
I watched three turtledoves eating in a cage
one of them white
one of them dyed pink
one pale blue
a coin in with their grain
pigeons watching from
the church windowsills
others flying overhead
some few bright clouds moving
all of it returns without a sound

FERRY PORT

We will be leaving now in less than a week
meanwhile we are
staying in a house in the port
helpful friends
have found us a top floor with a round balcony
like the plank roof of a tower
jutting over the corner of the back street
we sit out in the late afternoon
long grass and the trees of a park
on the far side
and a few cars on the hill
I try to imagine what it would be like
to live here
say for a winter
we go almost every day
to the library
and read about the island we are leaving
we walk around the harbor
the ferry building is the largest in town
new behind high wire fences
yellow tiles five storeys
blocking out the view of the harbor entrance
much larger and more solid
than the creaking wooden
sun-beamed ferry barns of my childhood
now removed
this one is like a government
which employs everyone
our car is ready to be loaded
we have scarcely unpacked
it will be strange to be on the mainland
as it is to be on the earth itself
we drove to the port on a Friday

we are to sail on a Saturday
the fat woman shorter than we are
whose house we are in
will stand in her red dress
with her arms around us
in the evening
under the girders in the smell of oil in the wind
asking us questions
and telling us that we have been here
a week and a day

THE BANQUET

Travelling north day after day
your eyes darken
and the roads become guides knowing
a further evening

white sky later and later
and one by one
houses with blue ceilings
painted every year
doors and windows from a childhood
that was yours
shrink
seen again years afterwards
for one moment late in the day
when there is no time

in that age you went home from school
to the room where the crystals
are lit now for the banqueters
raising their glasses

hours before the first star

SERVICE

You can see that
nobody lives in
castles like that
any more
thank God I suppose
and the castle gate house
has been turned
into a gas station
which is closed because
nobody comes to that
back street on a Sunday
a dog is tied to the front door
in the rain
all afternoon
trained to bark at footsteps
but not cars
the wet yellow roses sag
in the empty green
shadow-bricked gardens
white
curtains are drawn
on all the bay windows

SOME OF THE MASTS

I hear my feet resound on a wharf
echoed from other wharves
through the centuries
the fishing boats are all moored
in the evening
unlit against harbor dusk
the hulls darker already than the gray
photographs of them
ladders folded against
tall cranes for unloading
nets dangling from long hooks
no glitter from gulls' eyes
whirlpools of rope almost full
small waves rocking under the wharf
as I go on around the harbor
by daybreak they will all be at sea

NORTH WIND

In summer
come the old dreams of living on a boat
and walking home to it as the evening
is beginning
along a dry wagon road
bordered with poplars
between ripening fields
long ago
arm around a soft woman
and the dreams of upland stone houses
quaking at hand in cicada sound
and those of a cabin farther in the woods
with the forester's whole family for guides
and coming to hear a rushing stream
and the old man saying
Get down it's the north wind
and all of us lying down in the woods
for a while
thinking of the green cabin
that needs paint
but still has all the old furniture

ISLAND

After two years
we rowed to the island
before it got dark
some were still swimming
in the short summer
on the sand behind us
though the sun
had gone
the sound of far
splashing
carried over the quiet water
through the dripping
of the oars
on the island there was no one
only trees and
open twilit grass under them
no wind
birds already sleeping
but no stars no cloud
almost on the horizon
against a low line of evergreens
a cabin steamer passing
slowly between lakes
with its lights on
then as we were coming back
clear sky
long blue star falling

JUNCTION

Far north a crossroad in mud
new cement curbs a few yards each way
rain all day
two men in rubber boots
hurry along under one plastic
carrying loud radio playing music
pass tin shack surrounded by
broken windshields
paintings of north places
only hotel
has no name
no light to its sign
river from bridge long misted mirror
far houses and red boats float
above themselves in gray sky
martins were hunting
in the morning
over log jams by another shore
cold suppertime
thinking of hares in boggy woods
and footprints of clear water

REMEMBERING A BOATMAN

After sundown yellow sky beyond shadow mountains
range upon range in long twilight under few distant clouds
darkening pastures run into the bays
birds are already asleep high on unlit roan cliffs
straw light still flickers on the water
between two headlands in short summer
at last a long boat rowed by one man standing
appears slowly from behind a headland on the right
and starts across
too far away to hear the sounds of the wood
or see colors
a few times the wake turns up light
then I forget him for years

ASSEMBLY

Nomads gather in autumn
driving herds to the great auctions
of animals on the gold earth
by then there is blood in the trees
nights are already cold
daybreak white
some of them open stalls by the river
and hang up for sale
loose pelts of different animals
and fur garments stitched with sinews
at moments during the summer
in upland pastures among birds
some play instruments
others sing clapping their hands

OLD GARDEN

One year I seem to have started north many times
standing in a garden
looking at a mountain
over a wall
once I went to the sea and watched the red sun
rise from its peak
watched it set white in the sea veil
as the moon came up
nights I walked on wet sand
and swam looking up
days in palm leaf shadows
I listened
I came to a dry river
in late afternoon one time
place that I thought I knew
and found among stream-bed stones
one white clay dove
in some way broken
there was my father
I came to a full river
another time
between low shores at dusk
and as I crossed over
one bird flew calling
so that I could hear
but not words
that may have been my mother
that year
and one time I woke every morning on a hill
and wanted to remain there
on the way north through the mountains

THE FIG TREE

Against the south wall of a monastery
where it catches the first sun
a fig tree a shadowy fig tree
stands by the door
all around the flowing trunk
suckers grow
it is against
the law of the church to pull them out
nobody remembers why
tree roots older than the monastery

THE WINDOWS

Here is a child who presses his head to the ground
his eyes are open
he sees through one window
the flat gray ocean
upside down
with an arbor of islands hanging from it
all the way to the horizon
and he himself is hanging from nothing
he might step down
and walk on the old sky far down there
out to the clouds
in the far islands
he might step on the clouds where they have worn shiny
he might jump from cloud to cloud
he watches lights flash
on and off along the dark shores
and the lights moving among the overhead islands
he feels his head like a boat on a beach
he heard the waves break around his ears
he stands up and listens
he turns to a room full of his elders
and the lights on
blue day in the far empty windows
and without moving he flies

THE FALCONS

There were years when I knew
the flowers in the red stone walls

now in the courtyard where I have returned with you
we drink the wine of visitors
the temperature of the cellars

dusk is welling
out of the dried blood of the masonry
no hour remains on the sundial
by now the owls of the tower corners
are waking on their keepers' fists
but it is still day
out in the air
and three falcons appear there
over the courtyard

no feathers on heads or breasts
and they fly down to us
to our wrists and between them
then hover and perch just above us
keeping us in sight
waiting
they are waiting for us

this time they will come with us
when we leave the island
tonight for the rest of our lives

THE TRESTLE

A postcard held
by one white thumbtack
to the tan wallpaper
above my head
in a room I stood in as a child
showed in brown the view
once long ago from this
tall train bridge
trembling over the gorge
with the tracks far below there
where we have just been
by the glittering rapids
under the black trees
past the only inn
we see it from here
as it is now
painted
between the moving girders

TALK OF FORTUNE

I meet her on the street
she says she is away a lot but it was
actually when she was living here
she came home to the apartment house
which I have just left
and inside by the mail boxes
she found a small old
woman who seemed to be trying
to open the inside door
and looked as though she had been
crying or it could have been laughing
and they tried to talk but
the old woman could not
speak more than a few words
and yet she was well dressed
even old velvet
and when the door was opened for her
she would not go in
for anything
but kept smiling and asking for
something or somebody in
another language
and when she could not make herself
understood she gave
my friend a leaf and went
away and the next day
my friend found a lot of money

THE FOUNTAIN

An old woman from the country
who sells tickets for sex shows
and looks at the buyers' faces
gave a party
in her kitchen
for her family and their friends
many of whom she did not even know
and she served everybody
yellow cake and meringues
made from her own eggs
as she told the company more than once
and no bag feed she said
she fed them on
oh yes you do grandma
said the small boy whose bed was in the corner
look she said and opened the back door
to show the hens in the evening light
scratching around the fountain

SUN

Dark rain at
winter solstice
and in the morning

rosemary under clear sky
bird on south doorstep
poised like a stone

THE FLIGHT

—for Bruce and Fox McGrew

At times in the day
I thought of a fire to watch
not that my hands were cold
but to have that doorway to see through
into the first thing
even our names are made of fire
and we feed on night
walking I thought of a fire
turning around I caught sight of it
in an opening in the wall
in another house and another
before and after
in house after house that was mine to see
the same fire the perpetual bird

W. S. Merwin

W. S. Merwin was born in New York City in 1927 and grew up in Union City, New Jersey, and in Scranton, Pennsylvania. From 1949 to 1951 he worked as a tutor in France, Portugal, and Majorca. After that, for several years he made the greater part of his living by translating from French, Spanish, Latin and Portuguese. Since 1954 several fellowships have been of great assistance. In addition to poetry, he has written articles, chiefly for *The Nation*, and radio scripts for the BBC. He has lived in Spain, England, France, Mexico and Hawaii, as well as New York City. His books of poetry are *A Mask for Janus* (1952), *The Dancing Bears* (1954), *Green with Beasts* (1956), *The Drunk in the Furnace* (1960), *The Moving Target* (1963), *The Lice* (1967), *The Carrier of Ladders* (1970) for which he was awarded the Pulitzer Prize, *Writings to an Unfinished Accompaniment* (1973), *The Compass Flower* (1977) and *Opening the Hand* (1983). His translations include *The Poem of the Cid* (1959), *Spanish Ballads* (1960), *The Satires of Persius* (1961), *Lazarillo de Tormes* (1962), *The Song of Roland* (1963), *Selected Translations 1948–1968* (1968), for which he won the P.E.N. Translation Prize for 1968, *Transparence of the World*, a translation of his selection of poems by Jean Follain (1969), *Osip Mandelstam, Selected Poems* (with Clarence Brown) (1974) and *Selected Translations 1968–1978*. He has also published three books of prose, *The Miner's Pale Children* (1970), *Houses and Travellers* (1977) and *Unframed Originals* (1982). In 1974 he was awarded The Fellowship of the Academy of American Poets.